LOUISE PENNY:

Biography of a Canadian author of mystery novels

CHARLES OLIVER

TABLE OF CONTENT

CHAPTER 1

Who is Louise Penny?

Louise Penny, a prestigious Canadian creator, has cut a specialty for herself in the realm of secret fiction. Brought into the world on July 1, 1958, in Toronto, Canada, Penny's excursion from a radio personality to an honor winning creator is downright striking. Her composing style, portrayed by complex plots, distinctive portrayals, and a profound feeling of compassion, has caught the hearts of readers around the world. This extensive investigation dives into the life, works, and effect of Louise Penny, revealing insight into her exceptional commitments to the abstract world.

Louise Penny's early stages assumed a critical part in molding her viewpoint and establishing the groundwork for her future as an essayist. Brought up in a family that esteemed writing and training, Penny fostered a strong fascination with narrating since the beginning. Her folks, both eager readers, acquainted her with a different scope of books, encouraging an adoration for writing that would turn into a directing power in her life.

Penny's instructive excursion drove her to learn at Ryerson College in Toronto, where she improved her abilities in correspondence. Her encounters in the field of radio telecom permitted her to refine her story capacities, an expertise that would later track down articulation in her books. The impact of her experience in communicating is apparent in the musical rhythm and drawing in exchange that describe her composition.

The Gamache Series

Louise Penny's advancement accompanied the formation of Boss Assessor Armand Gamache, the focal person in her acclaimed secret series. The Gamache series, set in the made-up town of Three Pines in Quebec, has become inseparable from Penny's name. The main book, "Still Life," distributed in 2005, acquainted readers with the serene yet perplexing universe of Three Pines and laid out the establishment for a series that would traverse various volumes.

Boss Monitor Armand Gamache, a smart and compassionate criminal investigator with a propensity for tackling complex cases, immediately turned into a darling scholarly figure. Penny's capacity to mix profundity into her characters, uncovering their weaknesses and intricacies, put her books aside in the secret classification. With every portion, readers got themselves fascinated in the plot as well as put resources into the existence of the occupants of Three Pines.

The Charm of Three Pines

One of the interesting parts of Louise Penny's work is her making of Three Pines, an imaginary town that fills in as the setting for the majority of her books. Three Pines, with its particular occupants and pleasant appeal, has turned into a person by its own doing. The town's ideal setting gives a distinct difference to the dull secrets that unfurl inside its nation, making a nuanced and charming story dynamic.

Penny's striking portrayals transport readers to Three Pines, permitting them to drench themselves in its cobblestone roads, comfortable cabins, and warm boulangerie. The feeling of local area and interconnectedness that penetrates the town adds an additional layer of profundity to the narrating, causing readers to feel like they are essential for the very close local area.

Subjects and Themes

At the core of Louise Penny's books is a rich embroidery of subjects that investigate the human condition with subtlety and responsiveness. The Gamache series dives into complex issues like love, misfortune, recovery, and the quest for significance. Penny's capacity to join these subjects into the texture of her secrets lifts her work past the traditional limitations of the class.

One repeating theme in Penny's books is the investigation of craftsmanship and its extraordinary power. Whether crafted by the made up craftsman Clara Morrow or the verse of Ruth Zardo, workmanship fills in as a vehicle for self-disclosure and recuperating in the realm of Three Pines. This topical investigation adds layers of significance to the accounts, welcoming readers to ponder the job of imagination in the human experience.

Basic Approval and Grants

Louise Penny's commitments to the artistic world have not slipped through the cracks. Her books have collected far and wide basic recognition, acquiring her various honors and awards. The Agatha Grants, Anthony Grants, and the Arthur Ellis Grants are among the many distinctions given to her for different portions in the Gamache series.

One of the most esteemed acknowledgments came in 2013 when Louise Penny was granted the Request for Canada, one of the country's most noteworthy regular citizen praises. This qualification featured her artistic accomplishments as well as her effect on Canadian culture and narrating.

Worldwide Effect and Interpretation

While established in the Canadian scene, Louise Penny's allure stretches out a long way past public boundaries. Her books have been converted into numerous dialects, presenting Boss Controller Armand

Gamache and the universe of Three Pines to a different worldwide crowd. The widespread subjects investigated in her works, combined with the appeal of her characters, have added to the worldwide outcome of the Gamache series.

The worldwide acknowledgment of Louise Penny's books addresses the comprehensiveness of the human experience depicted in her accounts. Readers from various societies and foundations have figured out something worth agreeing on in the close to home profundity and validity that describe her composition.

Penny's media presence stretches out past the pages of her books. Interviews, public appearances, and cooperation in artistic occasions have permitted her to associate with readers and offer experiences into her inventive strategy. Her connecting with character and lucid conversations on the subjects investigated in her books have additionally charmed her to a wide crowd.

Past her composing profession, Louise Penny has been a promoter for different causes. Her public persona mirrors a pledge to sympathy, compassion, and the improvement of society. Penny's meetings and public articulations frequently address issues connected with emotional wellness, civil rights, and the significance of graciousness.

Her own encounters, including conquering individual difficulties, have molded her point of view on the force of strength and the human limit with respect to change. This credibility reverberates with readers who value the complexities of her fictitious people as well as the certified warmth and intelligence that she brings to conversations outside the domain of fiction.

Louise Penny remains as a scholarly illuminating presence whose effect stretches out past the domain of secret fiction. Her capacity to create convincing stories, foster complex characters, and investigate significant subjects has raised her to a place of conspicuousness in the scholarly world. The Gamache series, with its charming setting and essential characters, fills in as a demonstration of Penny's narrating ability.

Through Boss Monitor Armand Gamache and the inhabitants of Three Pines, Louise Penny welcomes readers on an excursion of thoughtfulness, compassion, and revelation. Her books engage as well as reverberate with an all inclusive human experience, making her a darling writer for readers of different foundations.

As Louise Penny keeps on enthralling readers with her abstract contributions, one can expect with energy the new secrets and experiences that she will divulge in the pages of her future works. In the great embroidered artwork of writing, Louise Penny's commitments sparkle splendidly, making a permanent imprint on the hearts and psyches of the people who leave on the artistic undertakings she so ably winds around.

CHAPTER 2

The Early life of Louise Penny

Louise Penny's early life, set apart by an adoration for writing and a supporting climate, assumed a critical part in molding the one who might later turn into a scholarly peculiarity. This investigation dives into the early long periods of Louise Penny, following the underlying foundations of her energy for narrating, her instructive excursion, and the impacts that laid the preparation for her celebrated composing vocation.

Family Foundation and Early Impacts

Louise Penny's childhood was moored in a family that esteemed training and human expression. Her folks, both energetic readers, imparted in her a profound appreciation for writing from early on. The home climate gave a rich ground to the maturing essayist, as she was encircled by books and urged to investigate the universe of words.

Her folks' impact went past the scholarly domain; they likewise presented her to a different scope of social encounters. This early openness to alternate points of view and accounts expanded Penny's perspectives and added to the wealth of her later narration. The reverberations of these developmental impacts can be followed all through her works, where topics of social variety and understanding resound.

Instructive Excursion and Early Pursuits

As a youthful understudy, Louise Penny's scholastic process turned into a channel for her expanding imagination. She sought after her schooling at Ryerson College in Toronto, where she improved her abilities in correspondence. It was during these early stages that Penny's enthusiasm for narrating tracked down an underlying outlet, making way for her later profession as a creator.

While at Ryerson, Penny fostered an interest in radio telecom. This decision of study not just gave her a stage to develop her story capacities yet in addition offered an extraordinary road to associate with crowds. The abilities she obtained during her time in radio would later demonstrate priceless as she deciphered her narrating ability from the wireless transmissions to the composed page.

The Impact of Broadcasting on Composition

Louise Penny's experience in radio telecom made a permanent imprint on her composing style. The rhythm, musicality, and capacity to connect with a group of people that she sharpened in the telecom world tracked down a characteristic progress into her story voice as a creator. The verbally expressed word, with its ability to charm and convey feeling, turned into an essential piece of her narrating tool stash.

The impact of broadcasting likewise imparted in Penny a sharp feeling of discourse. Her characters, frequently adulated for their credibility and profundity, participate in discussions that vibe veritable and reverberate with readers. This dominance of discourse, an expertise honed during her telecom days, adds to the vivid nature of her books, bringing readers into the complicated trap of connections that she winds around.

Early Vocation: From Broadcasting to Composing

Following her schooling, Louise Penny set out on a lifelong career in radio, at first working for the Canadian Telecom Organization (CBC). This period denoted the start of her expert process, where she kept on refining her narrating skills. While her telecom profession was a huge part in her life, the change from radio to composing fiction was a characteristic development.

Penny's choice to seek after a profession recorded as hard copy fiction was not without its difficulties. The shift from the promptness of radio to the lone undertaking of composing books required a recalibration of abilities and an act of pure trust. However, it was this progress that would at last prompt the making of Boss Controller Armand Gamache and the dazzling universe of Three Pines.

The Gamache Series: Another Section Starts

In 2005, Louise Penny acquainted readers with Boss Monitor Armand Gamache with her presentation novel, "Still Life." This obviously the start of the profoundly acclaimed Gamache series, which would turn into the foundation of her scholarly inheritance. The choice to dig into secret fiction, a class known for its many-sided plots and complex characters, displayed Penny's flexibility as an essayist.

The formation of Boss Monitor Armand Gamache, a person portrayed by insight, sympathy, and a commitment to equity, was a huge takeoff from Penny's prior interests. Be that as it may, it ended up being a masterstroke, as Gamache immediately turned into a darling figure in the scholarly scene. The outcome of "Still Life" established the groundwork for a series that would traverse various books, each adding layers of profundity to the person and the made up world Penny had created.

Three Pines: An Imaginary Safe house Comes to fruition

At the core of Louise Penny's books is the made up town of Three Pines, a quiet yet confounding setting that fills in as the scenery for a significant part of the Gamache series. The production of Three Pines was a purposeful and propelled decision, furnishing Penny with a material on which to paint her stories with rich detail and environmental appeal.

The charm of Three Pines lies in its ideal depiction, complete with cobblestone roads, eccentric occupants, and a feeling of local area that penetrates the story. The town, however fictitious, feels true and invigorated, a demonstration of Penny's capacity to mix her settings with a tangible feeling of spot. Three Pines turns out to be something other than a scenery; it turns into a person by its own doing, impacting the elements of the narratives that unfurl inside its nation.

Subjects of Three Pines: Impressions of Early Life

The subjects investigated in the Gamache series, a considerable lot of which spin around affection, misfortune, reclamation, and the quest for importance, reverberate with a profundity that proposes a special interaction for Louise Penny. The sympathetic and nuanced depiction of her characters indicates a significant comprehension of the human condition, conceivably molded by her own encounters and reflections on life.

The town of Three Pines, with its imaginative local area and embrace of innovativeness, mirrors the social openness and appreciation for artistic expressions imparted in Penny during her early stages. The investigation of craftsmanship as an extraordinary power, a common theme in her books, may likewise be followed back to the social impacts that molded her initial life.

Acknowledgment and Grants: Early Indications of Progress

The progress of Louise Penny's initial books didn't go unnoticed. "Still Life" not just denoted the start of the Gamache series yet additionally gathered the consideration of artistic pundits and acquired her the lofty Fresh blood Blade Grant for best first novel from the Wrongdoing Scholars' Affiliation. These early honors flagged the appearance of another ability in the secret class, making way for a lifelong that would be characterized by basic recognition and broad reader deference. The honors and acknowledgment got for her initial works established a strong starting point for the progress and development of her scholarly impression.

While Louise Penny's public persona is firmly connected with her artistic accomplishments, her own life has not been without challenges. The excursion from her initial long time to turning into a top rated creator is set apart by snapshots of versatility, self-awareness, and win over misfortune. Penny's transparency about her battles, incorporating fights with liquor addiction and the deficiency of her significant other, Michael, to dementia, adds a layer of genuineness to her public picture. Her capacity to defy and share these parts of her life adds to the certified association she lays out with readers. The subjects of versatility and the extraordinary force of human association, apparent in her books, reflect her own encounters and development.

As Louise Penny's scholarly vocation prospered, so did her obligation to generosity and backing. Her public assertions and meetings frequently address issues near her heart, including emotional wellness, mindfulness and the significance of sympathy in the public eye.

Penny's support work mirrors a sense of obligation to involve her foundation for positive change. Her contribution in beneficent drives and her eagerness to talk straightforwardly about psychological well-being add to a more extensive discussion about these significant issues. In doing as such, she broadens the topics of compassion and grasping present in her books into this present reality.

The Early Years as an Establishment for Significance

The early long periods of Louise Penny's life established the groundwork for an exceptional scholarly vocation. The impact of a family that esteemed writing, the instructive encounters that molded her relational abilities, and the progress from broadcasting to composing all assumed essential parts in forming the writer we know today. The making of Boss Overseer Armand Gamache and the captivating universe of Three Pines denoted a defining moment in Penny's vocation, catapulting her into the positions of globally acclaimed creators. The subjects investigated in her books, established in the human experience and improved by her own appearance, have reverberated with readers around the world.

As Louise Penny proceeds to compose and rouse, her initial years stay a standard for figuring out the underlying foundations of her imagination. From the comfortable bounds of her experience growing up at home to the wireless transmissions of radio telecom, every section of her initial life added to the embroidery of encounters that inject her books with realness, sympathy, and a significant comprehension of the human soul.

CHAPTER 3

The Personal life and relationship of Louise Penny: Marriage to Michael Whitehead

Louise Penny was hitched to Michael Whitehead, a recognized specialist and hematologist. The couple shared a coexistence, and their relationship was a huge piece of Penny's own excursion. While explicit insights regarding the early long stretches of their marriage may not be broadly reported, it is obvious that they framed areas of strength for a.

One of the most strong parts of Louise Penny's own life is the difficulties she confronted, especially the sickness of her significant other, Michael, and his possible passing. Michael Whitehead fought dementia, a staggering condition that influences the individual straightforwardly as well as negatively affects their friends and family. Penny's excursion as a parental figure during her significant other's sickness significantly influenced her and tracked down its direction into her later works.

The experience of seeing a friend or family member wrestle with dementia is a subject that reverberates in Penny's books, adding a layer of credibility and profound profundity to her depiction of connections and misfortune. In her meetings and public explanations, Penny has been open about the troubles she looked during this period and the close to home cost it took on her. Her eagerness to share such private encounters adds to a more profound comprehension of the lady behind the words and highlights the general subjects of affection, melancholy, and strength in her books.

Widowhood and Self-improvement

Following the death of her better half, Louise Penny explored the difficult territory of widowhood. The period after such a significant misfortune is in many cases a period of reflection, self-disclosure, and self-awareness. For Penny, this stage turned into a pot wherein she tracked down strength and versatility.

The subjects of flexibility and the groundbreaking force of self-improvement are obvious in her books, reflecting her imaginary people's excursions as well as her own. The Gamache series, with its investigation of human feelings and the intricacies of connections, turns into a material on which Penny paints her own encounters, implanting the stories with a feeling of fullness and weakness.

Artistic Impressions of Individual Encounters

Louise Penny's own life, incorporating her encounters with misfortune and sorrow, has filled in as a wellspring of motivation for her books. Boss Auditor Armand Gamache, the focal person in her books, wrestles with individual difficulties and misfortune, reflecting parts of Penny's own excursion. The person's profundity and close to home reverberation might be viewed as an impression of the creator's own route through the intricacies of life.

The made up town of Three Pines, with its affectionate local area and strong connections, repeats the significance of association and sympathy, esteems that probably acquired added importance for Penny during her own preliminaries. Through her composition, she makes convincing secrets as well as investigates the human condition with a profundity of figuring out that comes from lived encounters.

Tradition of Adoration and Misfortune in the Books

The effect of Louise Penny's own life on her books is a demonstration of her capacity to channel genuine feelings into her made up stories. The investigation of adoration and misfortune in the Gamache series isn't simply a scholarly gadget; it is Penny's very own impression of experiences with these significant parts of the human experience.

Readers, attracted to the genuineness of Penny's narrating, find comfort and reverberation in the depiction of characters who explore misery, remake their lives, and find new wellsprings of solidarity. The tradition of affection and misfortune implanted in her books makes a remarkable connection between the writer and her crowd, as readers see reverberations of their own delights and distresses in the pages of her books.

Emotional wellness Promotion

Notwithstanding her scholarly commitments, Louise Penny has turned into a backer for emotional well-being mindfulness. Her receptiveness about her better half's fight with dementia and her own difficulties, incorporating battles with liquor abuse, adds to destigmatizing these issues and cultivating a more empathetic comprehension of psychological wellness.

Penny's support work stretches out past the pages of her books, as she participates in open conversations, meetings, and occasions zeroed in on psychological well-being. Her readiness to share individual encounters is a strong power in separating boundaries and empowering others to look for help and backing.

Louise Penny's own excursion, set apart by affection, misfortune, and flexibility, has made a special association with her readers. The legitimacy with which she shares her encounters cultivates a feeling of closeness, as though readers are welcomed into the creator's inward world. This association goes past the scholarly domain, making a local area of readers who value the secrets woven into her books as well as the humankind that underlies them.

Through online entertainment, public appearances, and meetings, Penny keeps an exchange with her readership. The common encounters of satisfaction and distress, the festival of wins, and the affirmation of battles make a bond that rises above the customary writer-reader relationship. Along these lines, Penny's own life becomes entwined with the aggregate encounters of the people who track down comfort and motivation as would be natural for her.

The Lady Behind the Words

While Louise Penny is legitimately celebrated for her scholarly accomplishments, her own process adds a layer of profundity to the stories she makes. The affection she imparted to her late spouse, the difficulties she faced as a parental figure, and the versatility she found despite misfortune have all molded the writer behind the books.

Her transparency about private battles, incorporating her fights with liquor abuse and the effect of dementia on her family, adds to a more extensive discussion about human weakness and the strength that can rise up out of misfortune. In meshing these individual encounters into her books, Penny changes her aggravation into workmanship, making stories that reverberate with readers on a significant level.

As Louise Penny proceeds to compose and draw in with her crowd, her own life stays a wellspring of motivation for both her and the people who track down solace and association in her books. The lady behind the words arises as a narrator whose credibility, sympathy, and flexibility have made a scholarly heritage that rises above the limits of fiction.

CHAPTER 4

Louise Penny Career

Louise Penny, the skilled Canadian creator, has scratched her name into the records of contemporary writing with a dazzling vocation crossing secret books, each page a demonstration of her narrating ability and nuanced investigation of the human condition. This thorough investigation digs into the multi-layered features of Louise Penny's vocation, from her initial introductions to keeping in touch with the worldwide recognition earned by the Main Examiner Armand Gamache series, revealing insight into the development of a scholarly light.

Early Years and Change to Composing

Louise Penny's initial years were saturated with an adoration for writing cultivated by her loved ones. Her folks, devoted readers, imbued in her an enthusiasm for narrating that would later blossom into a surprising composing vocation. Regardless of her initial partiality for words, Penny left in an alternate proficient way at first, learning at Ryerson College in Toronto and later diving into radio telecom.

Her experience in radio telecom ended up being a developmental stage, leveling up her story abilities and imparting in her a particular musical rhythm that would later portray her composition. The change from broadcasting to composing fiction denoted a critical second, where Penny diverted her gifts to create stories that would reverberate with readers around the world. This shift laid the preparation for a scholarly excursion that would enrapture crowds and procure her basic praise.

The Introduction: "Still Life" and Boss Reviewer Armand Gamache

In 2005, Louise Penny left her permanent imprint on the abstract scene with the arrival of her presentation novel, "Still Life." This debut adventure not just acquainted readers with the beguiling town of Three Pines in Quebec yet in addition uncovered the perplexing Boss Assessor Armand Gamache. The original set the vibe for what might turn into an arresting series, laying out Penny as an expert narrator in the secret type.

Boss Investigator Armand Gamache arose as the key part of Penny's story universe, a person whose wisdom, empathy, and commitment to equity would become inseparable from the creator's name. Gamache's introduction denoted the start of a personal bend that would unfurl across a progression of books, every portion extending the intricacy of both the investigator and the secrets he confronted.

Three Pines: A Scholarly Safe house

Integral to Louise Penny's vocation is the making of Three Pines, a made up town that fills in as the background for the vast majority of the Gamache series. Three Pines, with its curious appeal, mixed occupants, and an apparently unspoiled setting, turned out to be in excess of a simple area; it turned into a person by its own doing. The town's appeal lies in its pleasant depiction as well as in the profundity of local area and interconnectedness that plagues its made up roads.

The decision of setting turns into a story gadget, permitting Penny to investigate the elements of local area, connections, and the human experience against the scenery of a quiet yet strange region. The town turns into a microcosm, mirroring the more extensive subjects and clashes that unfurl inside its nation, offering readers a feeling of commonality and inundation.

Complexities of Character: Making Boss Reviewer Armand Gamache

At the core of Louise Penny's prosperity lies her capacity to make characters that resound with readers on a significant level. Boss Overseer Armand Gamache, a focal figure in her books, remains as a demonstration of Penny's dominance of character improvement. Gamache's persona is layered with subtlety, epitomizing shrewdness, compassion, and an immovable obligation to equity.

As the series advances, Gamache's personality goes through huge development and change, mirroring the creator's expertise in winding around accounts that rise above simple wrongdoing. The intricacies of Gamache's connections, his conflicts under the surface, and the philosophical thoughts on life add to the persevering through allure of the series, causing readers to put in the secrets as well as in the characters' very own excursions.

Subjects and Themes: Unloading the Layers

One of the signs of Louise Penny's profession is her adroit investigation of topics that rise above the conventional limits of the secret type. The Gamache series digs into significant topics like love, misfortune, reclamation, and the quest for importance. These overall themes hoist her work past the limits of a regular wrongdoing novel, welcoming readers into a thoughtful and sincerely charged scholarly experience.

Craftsmanship, both visual and scholarly, arises as a repetitive theme in Penny's books. Crafted by the imaginary craftsman Clara Morrow and the verse of Ruth Zardo act as vehicles for self-revelation and thoughtfulness. Through these imaginative articulations, Penny instills her stories with a feeling of greatness, proposing that inventiveness can be a salve for the human spirit.

Basic Recognition and Grants: The Amazing Accomplishments

Louise Penny's abstract commitments have not slipped through the cracks, as proven by the various honors and awards that embellish her book reference. Her books have gotten acknowledgment from esteemed foundations, including the Wrongdoing Essayists' Affiliation, where she was granted the Fresh blood Knife for best first novel for "Still Life."

The Agatha Grants, Anthony Grants, and the Arthur Ellis Grants are among the many distinctions given to Penny for different portions in the Gamache series. The broad basic recognition addresses the persevering through nature of her narrating, solidifying her status as a light in the secret class.

Worldwide Achievement and Interpretation

While established in the Canadian scene, Louise Penny's effect reaches out a long way past public lines. Her books have been converted into various dialects, permitting readers from different societies to drench themselves in the realm of Boss Controller Armand Gamache. The widespread subjects investigated in her works, combined with the appeal of her characters, have added to the worldwide progress of the Gamache series.

The worldwide acknowledgment of Louise Penny's books is a demonstration of the comprehensiveness of human encounters depicted in her accounts. Whether in the clamoring cities of Asia, the quiet scenes of Europe, or the different networks of South America, readers have figured out something worth agreeing on in the profound profundity and realness that describe Penny's composition.

Media Transformations: The Gamache Series on Screen

The outcome of Louise Penny's books has normally started interest in carrying her accounts to different types of media. conversations and talks for film or TV variations of the Gamache series were progressing. The possibility of seeing Boss Assessor Armand Gamache and the inhabitants of Three Pines on screen has invigorated fans and is characteristic of the persevering through appeal of Penny's narrating.

A fruitful transformation wouldn't just acquaint Penny's work with a more extensive crowd yet additionally offer a visual understanding of the characters and settings that have become darling to readers. The potential for a screen variation highlights the immortal and culturally diverse allure of the Gamache series.

Past the pages of her books, Louise Penny has developed a public persona that resounds with readers. Her commitment with her crowd stretches out to virtual entertainment, meetings, and public appearances, where she shares bits of knowledge into her creative cycle, the motivation behind her accounts, and reflections on the subjects investigated in her books.

Penny's receptive and warm disposition, combined with her certified appreciation for her readership, has charmed her to fans around the world. The openness of the writer permits readers to feel associated with the imaginative psyche behind the secrets they eat up, cultivating a feeling of locality among the individuals who value her work.

Louise Penny's vocation isn't bound to the domains of fiction; it reaches out into the domain of individual reflections and support. Her receptiveness about her battles, incorporating her better half's fight with dementia and her own encounters with liquor addiction, adds a layer of vagueness to her public picture. By sharing these individual parts of her life, Penny adds to a more extensive discussion about weakness, versatility, and the significance of sympathy.

Her promotion work, especially in the domain of emotional well-being mindfulness, mirrors a promise to involve her foundation for positive change. By tending to trashed subjects and empowering discussions about emotional wellness, Penny broadens the topics of empathy and grasping present in her books into this present reality.

As Louise Penny keeps on writing secrets that captivate readers, her heritage in the scholarly world turns out to be progressively articulated. The Gamache series, with its complex plots, rich portrayals, and investigation of significant subjects, has made a permanent imprint on the secret sort. Her capacity to flawlessly mix the shows of wrongdoing fiction with scholarly profundity has impacted another age of journalists and raised the assumptions for readers.

The tradition of Louise Penny reaches out past individual books; it lies in the aggregate effect of a collection of work that has contacted the hearts and brains of readers universally. Her books are not simple redirections but rather windows into the intricacies of the human spirit, where secrets act as a focal point through which we look at our common encounters.

Planning ahead: The Unknown Secrets Ahead

Louise Penny's excursion as a creator proceeds, with the commitment of new secrets yet to unfurl. The expectation encompassing each new delivery confirms the getting through interest with Boss Overseer Armand Gamache and the imaginary town of Three Pines.

The direction of Louise Penny's vocation stays a story yet to be completely composed, a clear page anticipating the ink of future stories. Readers, old and new, enthusiastically anticipate the following part in the scholarly odyssey of a reshaped the creator scene of secret fiction, demonstrating that the charm of a very much created secret is immortal and vast.

The Embroidery of a Scholarly Illuminating presence

Louise Penny's vocation is a rich embroidery woven with the strings of secret, humankind, and scholarly dominance. From her initial days as a radio telecaster to turning into a universally acclaimed creator, Penny's process embodies the groundbreaking force of narrating. The making of Boss Examiner Armand Gamache and the town of Three Pines has turned into a standard for readers looking for secrets to tackle as well as reflections on life, love, and the flexibility of the human soul.

Through her characters, subjects, and individual reflections, Louise Penny has made a permanent imprint on the artistic world. Her work rises above the impediments of class, welcoming readers to set out on an excursion that goes past the unwinding of secrets to the disentangling of the intricacies inside ourselves.

As Louise Penny keeps on writing new stories and draws in with her readership, her vocation remains as a motivation for hopeful journalists and a wellspring of solace for the people who look for comfort in the pages of a very much created secret. The one who began her vocation with "Still Life" has developed into a scholarly illuminator, and the charm of her stories stays as strong as the secrets ready to be found inside the bounds of Three Pines.

CHAPTER 5

The Legacy and Impact of Louise Penny

Louise Penny, the illuminator of secret fiction, has made a permanent imprint on the artistic world with her Main Controller Armand Gamache series. As readers cross the overly complex plots of her books and explore the cobblestone roads of Three Pines, they experience not only secrets to be disentangled however significant investigations of the human soul. This broad investigation dives into the getting through heritage and significant effect of Louise Penny on the class, readership, and the social scene overall.

The Development of a Scholarly Inheritance

Louise Penny's inheritance is one manufactured through a consistent combination of scholarly craftsmanship, sympathetic narrating, and a resolute obligation to investigate the profundities of the human condition. Her vocation, spreading over various books and gathering worldwide recognition, has reshaped the secret class, raising it past ordinary wrongdoing fiction to a domain where secrets act as doors into the intricacies of life.

The Main Reviewer Armand Gamache series remains as the foundation of Penny's artistic inheritance. From the introduction novel, "Still Life," to the most recent portions, every section adds to an embroidery of interconnected secrets, character curves, and topical investigations. The heritage isn't just an assortment of books yet a story universe where the limits among fiction and reality obscure, welcoming readers to submerge themselves in the nuanced world Penny has carefully created.

Lifting the Secret Classification

One of the main commitments of Louise Penny's inheritance is her extraordinary effect on the secret classification. Generally portrayed by wrongdoing tackling stories with an emphasis on riddles and interest, the class has, through Penny's work, become a material for more profound investigation. The Gamache series rises above the bounds of whodunits, presenting components of artistic fiction, philosophical thoughts, and complex person studies.

Penny's books have extended the skylines of what secret fiction can accomplish. The complexities of the plots are matched by the close to home profundity of the characters and the significant subjects woven into the stories. In doing as such, she has re-imagined the assumptions for readers and individual writers the same, moving another flood of secret essayists who try to imbue their works with the sort of artistic wealth exemplified by Louise Penny.

Mankind In the midst of Secret: Topics of Sympathy and Compassion

At the center of Louise Penny's inheritance is her capacity to implant her secrets with a significant feeling of humankind. The topics of sympathy, compassion, and the flexibility of the human soul resound all through the Gamache series. The characters, confronted with difficulties and moral situations, explore the complexities of wrongdoing as well as the intricacies of connections and self-awareness.

Penny's investigation of human feelings, despondency, love, and recovery lifts her work to a level where readers get themselves engaged in settling secrets as well as sincerely put resources into the existences of the characters. The tradition of mankind in the midst of secret has set a norm for the class, welcoming readers to look for not simply the excitement of a very much created puzzle however the close to home reverberation that waits long after the last page.

Three Pines: A Legendary Sanctuary in Writing

The made-up town of Three Pines, with its comfortable bistro, beguiling houses, and mysterious charm, has turned into a legendary sanctuary inside the scene of writing. The making of Three Pines isn't just a setting; it is a person by its own doing, forming the elements of the stories and filling in as a mirror mirroring the human experience. The tradition of Three Pines lies in its capacity to rise above fiction, turning into a spot readers long to visit, if by some stroke of good luck in their minds.

Penny's striking portrayals transport readers to the cobblestone roads and warm hearths of Three Pines, summoning a feeling of sentimentality and solace. The town, however fictitious, has obtained a discernible reality in the personalities of readers, outlining the force of Penny's unmistakable ability. Its heritage is scratched in the pages of the books as well as in the aggregate creative mind of the people who have been shipped to its charming scene.

Character Profundity and Boss Reviewer Armand Gamache

The getting through tradition of Louise Penny is complicatedly attached to the profundity and intricacy of her characters, most remarkably Boss Overseer Armand Gamache. Gamache, with his astuteness, compassion, and devotion to equity, has turned into a notorious figure in the scholarly world. The person's advancement across the series, from the presentation in "Still Life" to ensuing portions, reflects the development and strength that characterize the human experience.

Gamache's inheritance reaches out past his job as an investigator; he encapsulates the characteristics of insight and empathy that readers see as significantly resounding. The person fills in as a scholarly standard, welcoming readers to mull over the secrets he disentangles as well as the significant subjects he wrestles with, from the intricacies of human connections to the idea of good and fiendishness.

Worldwide Recognition and Interpretation: A Worldwide Scholarly Impact

Louise Penny's effect rises above borders, proved by the worldwide approval her books have gotten. The Gamache series has been converted into various dialects, permitting readers from different societies to drench themselves in the secrets of Three Pines.

The worldwide reverberation of Penny's work highlights the general subjects and appealing characters that structure the bedrock of her artistic inheritance.

Global readers, whether in North America, Europe, Asia, or past, have settled on something worth agreeing on in the accounts made by Penny. The tradition of worldwide recognition positions her as a scholarly minister, exhibiting the force of narration to connect social partitions and interface readers across the globe.

Basic Praise and Grants: A Path of Scholarly Distinctions

The tradition of Louise Penny is interspersed by a path of scholarly distinctions and basic praise. Grants, for example, the Agatha Grants, Anthony Grants, and the Arthur Ellis Grants embellish her book reference, denoting every portion in the Gamache series as a work of excellent legitimacy. The acknowledgment from the Wrongdoing Authors' Affiliation, including the Fresh blood Knife for best first novel, highlights Penny's effect on the secret sort.

Basic praise not just commends the scholarly benefits of Penny's work yet in addition concretes her status as a pioneer in the class. The tradition of grants fills in as a demonstration of the getting through nature of her narrating, adding to the social and scholarly scene.

Media Transformations and the Visual Inheritance

The expectation encompassing likely film or TV variations of the Gamache series adds another aspect to Louise Penny's heritage. The possibility of seeing Boss Examiner Armand Gamache and the inhabitants of Three Pines on screen further expands the span of Penny's narration. Fruitful transformations wouldn't just acquaint her work with a more extensive crowd yet additionally offer visual translations of the characters and settings that have become darling to readers.

The visual inheritance, whether acknowledged through screen variations or the clear symbolism painted by Penny's exposition, improves the getting through effect of her accounts. The potential for visual narrating highlights the ageless and diverse allure of the Gamache series, getting its position in the more extensive social creative mind.

Drawing in with readers: The Living Heritage

A sign of Louise Penny's inheritance is her commitment with readers. Past the limits of the books, Penny effectively associates with her crowd through web-based entertainment, meetings, and public appearances. The living inheritance isn't bound to the pages of a book, however it stretches out to the continuous exchange between the writer and her readership.

Through communications, whether face to face or on the web, Penny cultivates a feeling of local area among her readers. The common experience of investigating Three Pines and diving into the secrets ties readers together, making a scholarly cooperation that rises above geological limits. The living heritage is a demonstration of the getting through association between a creator and the people who track down comfort and motivation in the most natural sounding way for her.

Support and Social Effect: Past the Composed Word

Louise Penny's inheritance reaches out past the domain of writing to support and social effect. Her transparency about private battles, incorporating her better half's fight with dementia and her encounters with liquor addiction, adds to destigmatizing these issues. The backing for psychological well-being mindfulness mirrors a promise to involve her foundation for positive change.

The effect of Penny's backing work reverberates in the more extensive social discussion encompassing emotional wellness. By tending to these disparaged subjects, she adds to a more humane and figuring out society. The tradition of social effect is a demonstration of the creator obligation that accompanies a conspicuous voice in the open arena.

Rousing People in the future: A Scholarly Legacy

As Louise Penny's vocation proceeds, her heritage turns into a scholarly legacy for people in the future of journalists and readers. The Gamache series, with its story intricacy and investigation of all inclusive subjects, sets a high watermark for hopeful creators trying to make secrets that rise above the class' shows.

The tradition of motivation is obvious in the endless readers who have been attracted to the Gamache series, starting their own adoration for writing and the craft of narrating. Trying essayists, affected by Penny's story ability, set out on their own excursions, looking to make works that leave an enduring effect on readers' souls and minds.

The Never-ending Reverberation of Louise Penny

Louise Penny's heritage is a never-ending reverberation in the scholarly world. Her effect on secret fiction, described by the rise of narrating to a work of art, has made a permanent imprint on readers, individual creators, and the social climate. The persevering through charm of Boss Investigator Armand Gamache, the legendary safe house of Three Pines, and the significant investigation of humankind in the midst of secret structure are the mainstays of a heritage that rises above the limits of time and geography.

As readers keep on uncovering secrets inside the pages of Louise Penny's books, they all the while uncover the persevering through tradition of a writer whose words have turned into a basic piece of the abstract standard. The one who acquainted us with Three Pines has turned into a scholarly illuminator, her inheritance a timeless fire that enlightens the ways of readers, journalists, and narrators on the way. The reverberation of Louise Penny's heritage isn't restricted to the past; it reverberates in the present and resonates into a future where secrets still need to be settled and stories long to be told.

Printed in Great Britain
by Amazon

40596575R00035